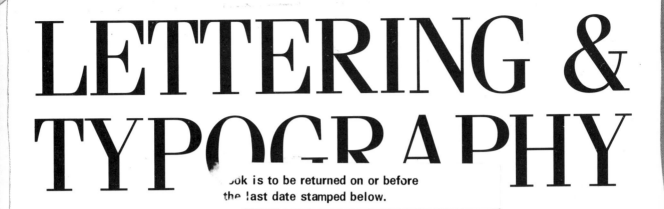

LETTERING &
TYPOGRAPHY

TONY POTTER

Designed by
IAIN ASHMAN

Lettering by
PATRICK KNOWLES

Alphabets designed by
**MICHAEL HARVEY,
JONATHAN COLECLOUGH & WILF DICKIE**

Illustrated by
STEVE CROSS

Additional illustrations by
**GUY SMITH, IAN JACKSON,
CHRIS LYON, COLIN RATTRAY,
PAUL BAMBRICK, JEREMY BANKS**

Contents

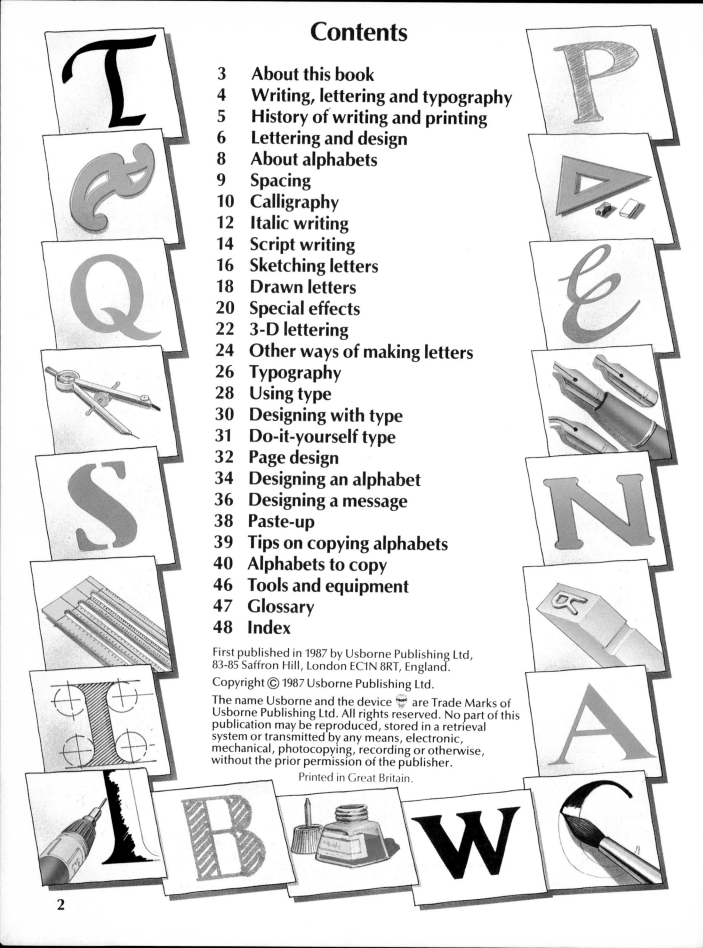

First published in 1987 by Usborne Publishing Ltd,
83-85 Saffron Hill, London EC1N 8RT, England.

Copyright © 1987 Usborne Publishing Ltd.

Printed in Great Britain.

About this book

This book is a practical guide to the making and use of letters, or letterforms. It covers letterforms made by hand and by machine, from writing to printing. It explains the basic techniques of both handmade and machine-made letterforms, which are summarized below.

The book is divided into six parts, identified by coloured stripes at the top of the page, like this:

The yellow, pink and green parts are all about hand-lettering methods.

First you can read about the history of lettering, from ancient cave symbols to the latest computerized methods. You can also find out about special words used to describe and organize letters.

Next you can find out how to do different styles of handwriting.

- **Calligraphy, which means "beautiful writing".** See page 10
- **Italic handwriting – a style of calligraphy.** See page 12
- **Different kinds of script writing.** See page 14

Various ways of drawing and painting letters are explained next. There are also tips on different ways of making three-dimensional letters.

- **Sketched letters** See page 16
- **Drawn letters** See page 18
- **Distorted letters** See page 20
- **3-D letters** See page 22
- **Stencilled letters** See page 24
- **Cut paper letters** See page 24
- **Rubbings** See page 25
- **Sprayed letters** See page 25

This part of the book is all about machine-made letters. The study of this is called typography.

- **Typesetting (like the words on the pages of this book).** See pages 26-29
- **Typewriting** See page 32
- **Rub-down lettering** See page 32

This part of the book gives lots of tips on design and layout. Layout is how letters and pictures are organized on a page. These tips are useful whether you want to use hand or machine-made methods to do posters, greetings cards, newsletters or any other kind of message which uses words.

Finally, there are some alphabets to copy. Tips on copying alphabets are on page 39.

Glossary

This book introduces many unusual words. These are defined on page 47 and are highlighted in the book on each page where you first come across them, like this: *pica*.

Design tips

Throughout this book there are tips on design to help you make the most of your lettering. You can find them easily by looking for headings in blue like this:

Getting started

Few tools or materials are needed to get started with lettering – just paper and a few inexpensive pens.

The styles of lettering shown in this book are not fixed styles that you must stick to rigidly. It is a good idea just to have a go at styles you are interested in as you come across them in the book and then practise as much as possible. You will probably find you quickly develop styles of your own, based on those explained.

Guide lines

For any hand-lettering, it is a good idea to draw guide lines in pencil, as shown round the heading above, to help keep your lettering straight.

On thin paper, you can draw guide lines on the back, making it easier to erase them without smudging the lettering.

Guide lines

Writing, lettering and typography

This page shows the main ways of hand-lettering – writing and drawing – and introduces methods used in *typography*.

Letters, numbers and other characters, whether hand or machine-made, are called letterforms.

Writing

Writing is the direct creation of cursive, or flowing, letterforms made with a pen, pencil, brush or similar tool. Writing that aims to be beautiful is called *calligraphy*.

Italic handwriting

Copperplate

Brush script

There are many different styles of writing and calligraphy. Three styles, produced with different writing tools, are shown above.

Drawn lettering

Drawn letterforms are sketched or carefully constructed. There are usually three basic stages involved, shown on the right.

1 First the letters are lightly drawn in pencil. These are called *construction lines*.

2 Each letter is then revised, often by tracing the pencil lines, and then filled in with ink or paint.

3 Finally, any imperfections are corrected with white paint and a brush or a technical pen.

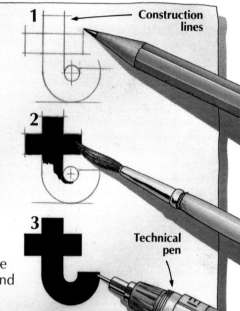

1 Construction lines

2

3 Technical pen

Type

Type is a letterform which has first to be drawn. It used to be cast in metal or cut in wood. Today, it is usually converted into electronic codes to produce a photographic image on paper.

The arrangement of type to form words is called typesetting.

Computer typesetting machine

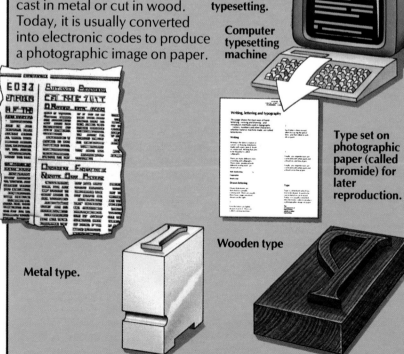

Metal type.

Wooden type

Type set on photographic paper (called bromide) for later reproduction.

Different type styles are called *typefaces*. Each complete alphabet, including numbers and punctuation marks, is called a *font* or *character set*.

1 abcdefghijklmnopqrstuvwxyz ABCDEFGHIJKLMNOPQRST 1234567890 .,;:''«»&!?

2 abcdefghijklmnopqrstuvwx ABCDEFGHIJKLMNOPQ XYZ 1234567890 12345678

3 abcdefghijklmnopqrstuvwxyz ABCDEFGHIJKLMNOPQRST 1234567890 .,;:''«»&!?

4 abcdefghijklmnopqrstuvw ABCDEFGHIJKLMNOPQR XYZ 1234567890 .,;:''«»&!?

Above are some popular type styles. See if you can identify them by looking at the tips on page 26.*

History of writing and printing

The history of the written and printed word is very complex. Below are some of the key developments in the western world.

20,000BC. Picture writing

Horse

Modern ideogram

Fish

Early realistic picture writing on cave walls gradually evolved into ideograms. These are symbols which represent ideas.

3000BC. Phonology

Cuneiform (from the Latin for "wedge") writing was pressed into clay with a wedge-like tool.

The first system with signs which represent sounds was used in the Middle East. This system of writing is called Cuneiform.

Ancient Greek writing

The Greeks adapted a Phoenician alphabet to create one of their own. Our alphabet is based on this.

The word "alphabet" comes from "alpha" and "beta", the first two letters of the Greek alphabet.

Ancient Roman writing

The Romans used the Greek letters A,B,E,H,I,K,M,N, O,X,T,Y,Z with few changes, added C,D,G,L,P,R,S and took three others (F,Q,V) from the Phoenicians.

Roman stone inscription.

Only capital letters existed at this time.

1st-15th centuries AD

During this time the modern alphabet, with large and small letters, gradually developed. Three extra letters (J,U,W) were added.

a b c d e o ʃ i m f p s t
ABEHIRLW

Pen-lettering

You can find out more about this period on page 10.

1450. Invention of type

Around 1450 Johann Gutenberg invented printing with movable type. Gutenberg's type was based on a style of handwriting popular at the time.

Page from Gutenberg's 42-line bible, about 1453-5.

1470. Roman typeface

The Venetian printer Nicholas Jenson, designed the first truly Roman *typeface*.

es naſcitur)ſed n
tur. Credidit eni

Jenson's typeface, which he designed in Venice.

Hand-made books

Monks in a medieval scriptorium.

Until printing was invented, books and other documents were produced in "scriptoria" – rooms full of scribes who copied pages by hand.

19th century

Hot metal typesetting machine

UNRIVALLED AT
ADMISS
ONE-SHI

Advertising typeface

Many new typefaces were designed, especially for advertising in the early 19th century. New machines to set type were invented later.

20th century. Computers and calligraphy

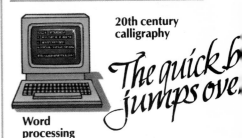

20th century calligraphy

The quick b jumps ove

Word processing

Computer typesetting and word processors were invented. There was also a revival of interest in pen lettering and calligraphy.

Lettering and design

Letters are the building bricks of words and messages. What they look like, how you organize them, and their suitability for the job are the three most important things in getting a message across successfully to someone. The choice of lettering depends on the purpose of what you have to say, the people you are saying it to and where it is said.

Appearance

The appearance, or style, of lettering communicates something, just as the words themselves do, as you can see below. Style is important because it affects the interpretation and effectiveness of what you are trying to say.

Message makers

DANGER

SAFETY HELMETS MUST BE WORN BEYOND THIS POINT

Warning signs need to be clear and easy to read.

Letters have two jobs. They are both symbols which have a meaning and decorative, or abstract, shapes. In this message, the meaning of the words is more important than their abstract shapes.

Here, letters make an abstract picture, but carry no precise message. In most graphic design, the meaning of the words and their appearance are equally important.

Letters are rarely used for decoration only.

Letters are usually used to form words to say something to someone.

If you needed driving lessons, which of these two schools would you choose from their advertisements? Try asking ten people the same question and you will probably find they go for the one on the right. The lettering looks calmer and more technical than the one on the left, making you feel confident about the school.

Similar lettering, used in another situation, has a different effect. Which sign do you think makes the vegetables looks the fresher? The lettering on the left looks "hand-made", thus making them seem more homely and genuinely fresh than the other sign does. You could ask ten people the same question to see if they agree.

Stages in design

Organizing messages is an important part of design. The steps on the right show the basic stages involved. Before starting you need to ask what you want to say and to whom? Is your message for young or elderly people? Is it to be read close by or at a distance as people dash past? Should it look "traditional", "modern" or "flashy"?

You can find out more about planning and designing messages on pages 32-33 and 36-37.

1 Copy

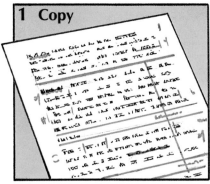

Words to be lettered or typeset are called *copy*. Copy often needs to be divided into chunks of words according to their relative importance.

2 Thumbnail

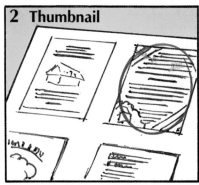

Thumbnails are tiny sketches, drawn in proportion to the full-size job, to work out various ways of arranging the information.

3 Rough

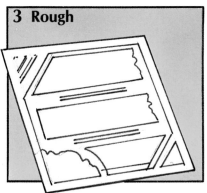

Designers often re-draw successful thumbnails to full size, adding colour if appropriate. This helps in refining the final idea.

4 Visual

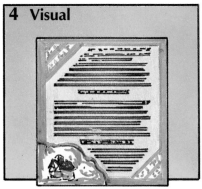

A visual is a well worked-out design, in colour if necessary, which gives a good idea of the finished work to show to a customer, or client.

5 Finished work

This is the finished work, ready to use, either as it is, or for subsequent printing. Finished work ready for printing is called *artwork*.

DESIGN TIPS

Organization

One of the aims of design is to achieve visual order. This means making your message clear to read and good to look at. There are several ways of achieving visual order within a block of copy, as described on the right. You can find out more about visual order on pages 30 and 37.

Copy which lines up on one side only is called unjustified.

This is ranged (or flush) left.

This is ranged (or flush) right.

Copy which lines up on both sides is called justified or flush left and right. Justified setting is nearly always used in newspapers.

This arrangement is called centred.

Words shaped around a picture have a ragged edge and are called run-arounds.

Run-arounds are often used in advertisements.

About alphabets

An alphabet is all the letters, numbers, punctuation marks and other characters used in a particular language. There are thousands of different styles of letterforms, used in books, papers, on signs, TV and so on.

abcde

Each letter in an alphabet is designed to look different from the others and yet form part of a whole. One letter slightly different in style from the rest stands out, as you can see above.

Letters are made to look part of a whole by designing them with certain features in common. A name is given to each of their parts, which helps designers to think and talk about them. You can find out the most important of these names on the right.

Changing any part circled in red, even by a tiny amount, would alter the letter's character.

Parts of letters

A font consists of capital letters (or upper case), small letters (or lower case), numbers, punctuation marks, and sometimes italics and small capital letters (which are the same height as the small letters).

Letters have basic parts, with special names, shown on the right.

Upright letters are also called roman.

Slanted letters are called italic.

Curve. Any curved shape.　Bowl. Continuous curve.

Serifs

Stem. Stroke running from top to bottom.　**Arm. Horizontal or diagonal strokes.**　**Bar. An arm joining two parts together.**

Serifs

Serifs are strokes which finish off the ends of stems, arms and curves. A letter without serifs is called *sans serif* (or sanserif).

Serifs derive from the use of brushes and chisels and often become distinctive features of letters. Other names

Serif

Sans serif

Many serif styles have evolved since Roman times. Some of the most common are shown below.

Full bracketed　Hairline　Slab　Slab bracketed

Head　Terminal

Ascender　Ascender line

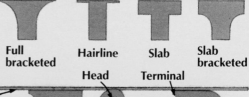

Descender　Base line　Descender line　Foot　Tail　"x" height

History of the alphabet

The ancient Roman alphabet of 23 letters, which forms the basis of the modern alphabet, was often cut on stone. The most beautiful of these inscriptions is thought to be that at the base of Trajan's column in Rome.

Inscription at the base of Trajan's column 113-114AD. A large proportion of the Roman population could read and there were informal styles of writing on vellum and parchment.

An alternative alphabet of small letters did not begin to appear until around the end of the 8th century AD, in a style called the Carolingian minuscule.

Spacing

Without spaces, lettering or type is very difficult to read, as you can see below.

ALLTHEBOOKSINTHEENGLISH
LANGUAGEHAVEBEENWRITTEN
WITHJUSTTWENTYSIXLETTERS.

There are three kinds of spacing to take into account when doing any kind of lettering: letter spacing, word spacing and line spacing.

Word spacing

Word spacing is the space between words.

GOOD WORD SPACING

Leave a space the size of a small "n" between words in small letters.

mallnlett

Leave a space the size of a large "O" between words in large letters.

RGEOLET

For *justified* text, as shown on the right, leave gaps of varying sizes between the words, not the letters.

> I must go down to the sea again, to the lonely sea and the sky, I left my shoes and socks there, I wonder if they're dry?

Letter spacing

Letter spacing is the space between letters. For lettering to look right, all gaps between letters must appear equal in size, although they may not actually be so.

This is a letter space.

FA

Well spaced word.

HELLO

Badly spaced word.

HELLO

You can judge by eye whether letter spacing is right by shading trial lettering as shown below.

HELLO

All shaded areas should look equal by eye.

Letters with adjacent vertical strokes need the greatest space between them.

Letters with adjacent curved or diagonal strokes need the least space.

The space needed between letters with open sides can be judged by drawing a line into the letter from which to shade in, as shown on the right.

You can leave as much or as little space as you like between letters, provided the spacing looks equal.

Ignore the *ascenders* and *descenders* when shading between small letters.

CST

GOODBY

GOODBYE

alc

Line spacing

Line spacing is the space between two consecutive ▶ lines of lettering or type.

Some designs look right with ▶ very tight line spacing, with ascenders and descenders touching.

Other designs look best with ▶ greater line spacing. Line spacing should be measured from one base line to another.

osaurus had three brains, though none of them were very big. It had one

know that the vented before he tin opener

ig. It had one ead, one in its ne in its back.

In general, the longer the line ▶ the greater the line spacing should be. Varied line spacing adds interest to lettering.

Today trip to holida delux ten m likel year from bing sno high ma at t

Today's trip to Flo holiday lo deluxe dec With over te you're likely three years of What more cou are over two re mornings by arr amongst th

Calligraphy

The word *calligraphy* comes from the Greek "kallos" meaning beautiful and "graphos" meaning writing.

Some experts claim calligraphy is a performance, like music and dancing – a skill that depends on practice and conveying feeling to look good. Others simply think of it as beautiful writing.

Many styles of calligraphy are used today, but most have their roots in old styles written with a broad nib.

The thick and thin strokes of the alphabets on this page result from using a broad nib, kept at a constant angle.

Square capitals

Ancient Roman square capitals
Square capitals, or Quadrata, were the broad pen versions of roman capitals, and were used for books and important documents. This style is considered very elegant and formal.

Rustic capitals

Ancient Roman rustic capitals
Rustic capitals were used by the Romans and are based on square capitals, but are more condensed and less formal looking. This became the main book hand.

Uncials

Uncials
Uncials developed from square capitals and were used as a book hand by the Romans and early Christians. The letters were often 1 inch high, for which the Roman name was "uncia".

Half-uncials

Half-uncial
The half-uncial were so called because they were often half an inch high. They are similar to uncials, except there are longer extensions above and below the body of the letters.

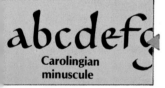

Carolingian minuscule

Carolingian minuscule
Charlemagne, king of the Franks (France and part of Germany) standardized writing with a style called Carolingian minuscule – the first small letters. He also introduced spacing between words on a regular basis.

Gothic

After minuscule hands
After Charlemagne, different versions of the minuscule were developed. One of these was called Textura, because it is so closely written that a page of it resembles woven cloth.

Italic script

Humanist scripts
New styles of writing, called Humanist scripts, were developed in Italy during the Renaissance. You can find out how to do one of these, called italic writing, over the page.

The lost art
By the late 19th century the art of writing with a broad nib was virtually lost. Handwriting was done with a pointed steel nib and thick and thin strokes made by exerting pressure.

Victorian lettering artists tried copying old styles, but most did not realize that the shape of the letters was made by the angle of a broad nib.

This style, done with a thin nib, was fashionable in the 19th century.

◄ Edward Johnston

In the 1890s Edward Johnston studied old manuscripts and re-discovered how the letterforms were written. He designed a basic alphabet, called the Foundation Hand, based on a form of writing used at Winchester in the 10th century.

Foundation Hand

Illuminated manuscripts

Many manuscripts, from medieval times and before, were beautifully decorated, or "illuminated", with patterns, pictures and elaborate borders, sometimes in gold.

Page from an illuminated manuscript.

Decorated initial letter

Many old manuscripts have decorated initial letters, like the one above. These seem to be saying, "start here", as well as adding decoration. You could use the same principle in your own lettering.

Modern calligraphy

Today, calligraphy is most often used where decorative effect is important.

Decorative alphabet

It is often used for book covers, invitations and greetings cards.

Poetry

Poems

Invitation

You are Invited to a WEDDING

Book cover

THE GREAT FIRE

Greetings card

Have a very Happy Birthday

Limbering-up

Calligraphy depends upon the flow and rhythm of a pen or brush rather than being drawn. Before starting something important calligraphers often find it useful to limber-up in order to get in the right frame of mind.

Changing nib angle

Try altering the nib or brush angle to see what happens to the shape of letters.

ABCDE
Horizontal

ABCDE
45°

ABCDE
90°

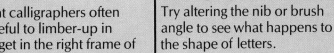

DESIGN TIPS

Contrast

Any message can be made more interesting to look at by including a contrast between the parts, called design elements. The pictures on the right show some of the different elements that you can contrast, either singly or together. Experiment with different combinations.

ABCDEF GHIJKLMNOPQ OPQRST
Size

ABCDEFG NOPQRS HIJKLMN
Style

ABCDE MNOPQ TUVWX
Weight

ABCDEFG HIJKLMNOPQ RSTUVW
Size & weight

HIJKLM PQRST TUVWX
Colour

BCDEF GHIJK LMNO
Position

Italic writing

In fifteenth century Italy, new styles of writing developed, including what is today called the italic hand. It is now a popular style of *calligraphy*, quick enough to be used for everyday writing.

Use the examples on these pages as a starting point. Copy them first, using guide lines (see page 3), then let a style of your own develop as you write more quickly.

Italic pens

There are lots of specially made italic pens you can buy.

Left-oblique nib

For italic writing you need a pen with a square-shaped nib. Learning is easiest with as broad a nib as you can get. If you are left-handed you may need a left-oblique nib, as shown above.

Nib angle

Hold the nib at 45° to the guide lines, keeping it at the same angle as you form the letters.

Draw a vertical cross with your pen to help get the angle right. Both parts of the cross will be the same thickness if you have the nib at 45°.

Proportions

Use the proportions shown below to draw your guide lines. Guide lines are not necessary for everyday writing, except to begin with.

Small letters

Capitals
7 pen widths

Adg

5 pen widths

Small letters

Build up your confidence by copying the small letters below in the order shown. (The alphabet is divided into groups of similar shaped letters.) Try writing individual letters over and over, then try a complete alphabet before writing words.

In italic writing letters should slant forwards slightly (about 5°).

These marks show the height of letters in pen nib widths.

o e c a g b d

p q i j n m h r u

v w x y z s l k f t

Joining letters

Many letters in italic writing can be joined up to make words, so that the writing flows and can be done quickly.

The quick brown fox jumps over the lazy dog

Joined-up letters

There are two kinds of joins – diagonal and horizontal. You will find out for yourself which letters are best left unjoined, but here are a few tips:

eo	*nm*	*dgqa*	*bp*
These letters can be joined from both sides.	These letters are best joined from the right only.	Avoid joining onto the left of these letters.	Avoid joining onto the right of these letters.

Capitals

Capitals in italic writing are quite similar to ancient Roman capitals (see page 8). The style of the basic capital letterform can be varied a great deal by adding decorative strokes, called flourishes. Letters like this are sometimes called swash capitals.

The alphabet to copy and learn below shows a basic version of each letter (for ordinary use), along with a decorative version of it.

(see page 8)

Writing a letter

Here are some tips on laying out a letter.

Margin proportions

Too small   Too large   Pleasing to look at.

Alternative layouts for letter headings.
▼

Alternative layouts for envelopes.
▼

History

In fifteenth century Italy new writing styles developed, called Humanist scripts. Their capitals were influenced by Roman letters and the small letters by an earlier style called Carolingian minuscule. This was the beginning of italic writing as known today.

Carolingian minuscule

Around 1523 Arrighi published a printed manual in Rome for people to copy from. His copy-book was influential throughout Europe.

Tips on spacing

Try not to pack letters too closely together as it makes words difficult to read. But beware – if the letters are too wide, the shape of the words may be lost.

| Too close | *tight* | Correct | *Spacing* |

Allow the space of a small letter "o" between words.
Word spacing

Leave a space two small "o"s high between the "x" height guide lines.
grey deal

Page from a printed copy-book. ↗

Script writing

Script is a term loosely applied to a number of informal writing styles often used for display purposes. There are no strict rules about how it must be done, except that it must be legible. Try copying the styles on these pages and then see if you can invent your own.

Greetings card

Different styles of script writing

Shop sign

Poster

Pens

Any kind of pen can be used for script lettering. There are also special script pens, with round or square-shaped nibs which lay flat on the paper. These give a constant stroke thickness, needed for styles like "script *sans serif*", shown on the right.

Round-tipped felt pens also give a constant stroke thickness.

These are called "Speedball" nibs, but other makes are available.

"B" series nibs are round and keep the same weight of line.

"C" and "D" series nibs make thick and thin strokes.

"A" series nibs are square and make strokes of the same weight.

Pointed nib for fine script.

Script sans serif

aAbBcCdDeEfFgG
hHiIjJkKlLmMnN
oOpPqQrRsStTuUvV
wWxXyYzZ

Try to keep these letterforms very rounded, with short ascenders.

Informal script

abcdefgh
ijklmnopqrsstu
vwxyz3

This is based on ordinary writing, with added flourishes. Try to join the letters in a smooth, unbroken line.

Techniques

abcde

Erase line when finished.

Instead of using guide lines, draw a pencil line and write across it as shown. Script often looks best if the letters appear to "dance", but with the body of the letters kept on a constant centre line.

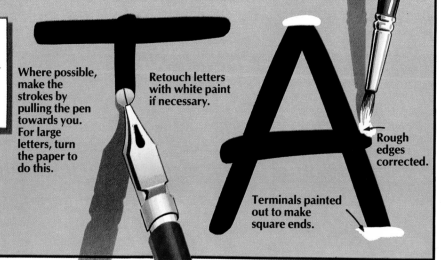

Where possible, make the strokes by pulling the pen towards you. For large letters, turn the paper to do this.

Retouch letters with white paint if necessary.

Rough edges corrected.

Terminals painted out to make square ends.

Brush lettering

Script letters drawn freely with a brush have a distinctive style of their own, but need lots of practice to get right.

Use a pointed watercolour brush, held so that you use its side.

The more pressure you use, the wider the stroke will be.

Practise these two strokes.

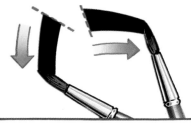

Pompeii

Roman street notices and graffiti painted by brush were found in Pompeii, in Italy, preserved by the volcanic ash which destroyed the town in 79AD.

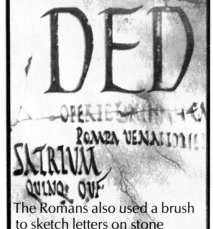

The Romans also used a brush to sketch letters on stone before carving them.

Eastern writing

In the East, brushes have been used for thousands of years to produce beautiful calligraphy. The picture below shows part of a Chinese message.

In Chinese, each character is a single word.

Chinese is read vertically, and from right to left.

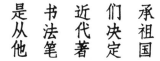

是 书 近 们 承
从 法 代 决 祖
他 笔 著 定 国

In China, fine handwriting is seen as a mark of respect.

You can buy Chinese brushes from some art shops to use for brush lettering. The brush is held vertically, and controlled by the thumb, index and middle fingers.

This is called the Ping Wan grip.

Block of Chinese ink

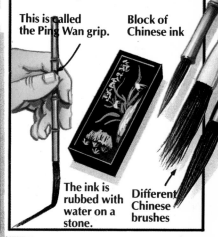

The ink is rubbed with water on a stone.

Different Chinese brushes

Brush lettering alphabet

ABCDEFGHIJKLM
NOPQRSTUVWXYZ
1234567890

You can copy almost any style of lettering with a brush, but this one is good to practise with.

DESIGN TIPS

Cut and paste

It is often very difficult to make script lettering look right – a message may look fine overall, but be spoilt by a few characters.

You can overcome this problem by writing lots of versions and then using a technique called "cut and paste" to combine the best parts of each.

This technique is also suitable for other styles shown in this book.

1

Write your message several times, at the same size.

2

Paste the strips together as shown, taking care to get the spacing right.

3

Choose the best parts and cut them into strips.

4

Photocopy the page and, if necessary, paint out any cut marks and photocopy again.

Sketching letters

You can create letters quickly in almost any style by sketching them – either by copying an alphabet* or by learning a style. These pages show some methods for roughing out ideas for anything from a poster to a record sleeve, and for creating lively letters for finished work. Sketching also helps you to understand the shape of each letter, and forces you away from your normal handwriting style. To start with, it is a good idea to copy and learn roman capitals, shown on the opposite page.

Sketching methods

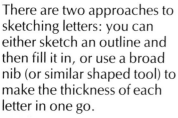

Filled-in outline.

Outline

Broad nib

Thin nib

There are two approaches to sketching letters: you can either sketch an outline and then fill it in, or use a broad nib (or similar shaped tool) to make the thickness of each letter in one go.

Sketching tools

Almost anything that makes a mark will do for sketching.

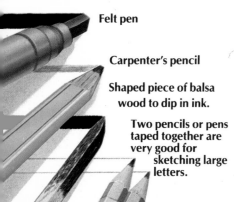

Felt pen

Carpenter's pencil

Shaped piece of balsa wood to dip in ink.

Two pencils or pens taped together are very good for sketching large letters.

Broad-pen sketching

You need to hold a broad nib pen (or similarly shaped tool) at a constant angle to make thick and thin strokes on each letter. The angle varies from style to style, but for upright capitals, like those on the opposite page, you need to hold the pen at between 30°-45° to the horizontal.

1
Hold the pen as shown below.

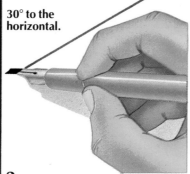

30° to the horizontal.

2
Keep your hand and the nib at the same angle while you form the letter.

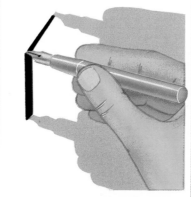

Try to move your hand with a smooth, flowing action.

Outline method

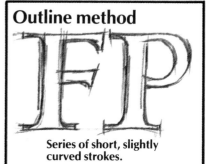

Series of short, slightly curved strokes.

By keeping your hand stationary on the paper and using the natural movement of your fingers, you can sketch outline letters like those above. You can then fill in the outline if you prefer.

1
Keep your hand still and move your fingers as shown below to make horizontal or vertical strokes.

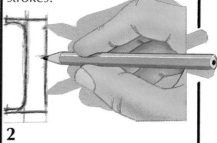

2
Sketch rounded strokes by moving your fingers as shown below.

There are alphabets to copy on pages 40-45.

Adding serifs

You can finish your letters by adding *serifs* with a pointed pen or pencil as shown below.

Imagine circles forming the outline of serifs, as shown below.

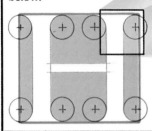

Serifs should be about a quarter of the circle and should appear to grow out of the stem of the letter.

Guide lines

Before sketching letters in any style, it helps to draw guide lines on your paper to help get the correct proportion of height to width of each letter.

1 For roman capitals, guide lines should be about nine times the thickest part of the letter.

2 If you are using a pen, measure the height by marking with the nib like this.

Roman capitals

The letters shown below are grouped according to their shape. Sketch each stroke slowly and deliberately, in the order shown by the arrows. It is a good idea to practise with a phrase like "The quick brown fox jumps over the lazy dog", as it includes all the letters of the alphabet.

Square graph paper is useful for sketching, as the squares help to get the letters in proportion.

All curved letters overlap the guide lines slightly, top and bottom. This makes these letters look as though they line up properly with others in a word – the result of an optical illusion.

The upper parts of an S and B are slightly larger than the lower parts.

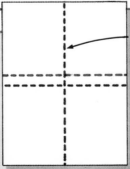

Balance

All the parts of a well-designed layout should balance. You can get a layout to balance either symmetrically or asymmetrically. A symmetrical layout is said to balance when there is an even distribution of visual weight on each side of its horizontal and vertical axis. Visual weight is not something you can measure, but something you have to see.

The vertical axis is an imaginary line down the middle.

The position of this line will depend on the visual impact of the words above and below it.

The true horizontal axis is an imaginary line across the centre. Because of an optical illusion, a line above this is the one used to balance the layout.

A symmetrical and an asymmetrical layout are shown below. In general, symmetrical layouts are easier to handle.

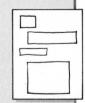

Symmetrical layout

Asymmetrical layout

You can use either approach in anything you design.

Drawn lettering

Lettering can be carefully drawn or painted, rather than being written directly with a pen. There are four main stages involved, explained on these pages. You may find the alphabets on pages 40-45 helpful if you want a style to copy.

1st stage — Pencil rough

There are several ways of drawing the basic outline: by construction, sketching or tracing.

Construction

There is an alphabet like this to copy on page 44.

Letterforms can be carefully measured and lightly drawn out in pencil using a T-square and set square.

Sketching

Sketch the style you want, as explained on pages 16-17.

Tracing

Trace the letters you want from an alphabet, then enlarge or reduce them using one of the methods shown on page 39.

2nd stage — Filling in

Fill in the outline with colour or black ink. Some examples are shown below.

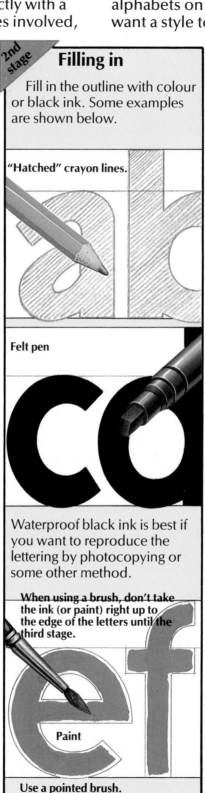

"Hatched" crayon lines.

Felt pen

Waterproof black ink is best if you want to reproduce the lettering by photocopying or some other method.

When using a brush, don't take the ink (or paint) right up to the edge of the letters until the third stage.

Paint

Use a pointed brush.

3rd stage — Outline

Next you may need to finish the outline, smoothing the edges and removing any unevenness left from the previous stage.

When drawing geometrical letterforms a ruling pen, used with a ruler as a guide, is good for crisp ink lines. These are quite difficult to use, so you need to practise beforehand.

Technical pen

You could draw outlines freehand, especially for curved parts.

Be careful when using Indian ink as it takes several minutes to dry.

Run the metal part of the brush along the ruler.

A fine brush is a good tool for finishing outlines, with a ruler as a guide, tipped back a little as shown.

Retouching

Use white paint* and a fine brush to tidy up any imperfections. This is called retouching. If your work is for reproduction (printing or photocopying), any retouched parts will not show when printed.

You may need to do a lot of retouching if you draw the outline freehand.

Drawing curved parts

The drawing instruments shown below are useful aids for drawing curved parts of letterforms.

French curves

Find the part of the curve nearest to the one you want and use it as a guide.

Flexible curve

Bend the curve to the shape you want.

Constructing serifs

For roman lettering, *serifs* can be constructed using a pair of compasses, as shown below.

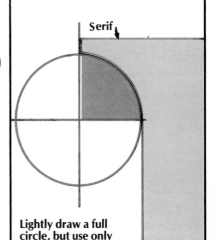

Serif

Lightly draw a full circle, but use only a quarter for the serif.

Drawing "straight" parts

The stems of many letterforms curve inwards slightly. An optical illusion actually makes them look straight. You will need to take this into account when drawing most non-geometric letters.

A B
abc

The typeface used in this book, called Optima, has curved stems as a deliberate effect.

You could use a ruler as a guide and tilt the pen as you draw to make a slight curve.

2 When drawing freehand, first draw a straight pencil outline, then use this as a guide for drawing a slight curve.

Spacing

Here is how to work out the length of lines of lettering to fit in a certain space.

1 At the sketch stage, sketch the lettering in lines, the width of your paper. Then cut the lettering into strips.

YOU ARE INVITED TO A PARTY AT 7.00 PM —

Paste the strips **2** onto a piece of paper, in the position you want them.

YOU ARE
INVITED
TO A PARTY
AT
7.00 PM

3 Trace off the lettering onto another piece of paper, ready for rendering.

Tracing

Designers often make a series of tracings of a drawing, improving each one bit by bit as they go.

1

Start with a sketch.

2

Place tracing paper over the sketch and trace over it, improving the parts you don't like and keeping the parts you do.

3

Continue using the last drawing to trace from, until you have a perfect copy.

*Special paint called process white is available for this.

Special effects

There are many ways of distorting letters to create special effects. For example, you can make lettering work both as a word and as a picture of the word, like this:  Some ideas are shown here, but you can probably think of more.

1 Draw the words in black ink on a piece of paper.

2 Crumple the paper, open it out, and take a photocopy of it.

3 Trace the lettering from the photocopy, enlarging it if needed.*

4 Carefully render the finished tracing with ink or paint.

1 Draw the words between guide lines on a piece of paper.

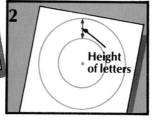

Height of letters

2 With a pair of compasses, draw two circles as shown.

Mark where each letter goes when the spacing looks right.

3 Cut up the letters and lay them around the circle.

Tracing paper

Pen

4 Lightly glue the letters, then trace them. Render the finished letters.

Perspective

There are two main ways of drawing letters in perspective, to give the illusion of depth: single and two-point. Both methods are explained here.

You can create good effects by pasting perspective lettering over backgrounds from magazines.

Single-point perspective

Use this method to make letters appear to be facing you in 3-D.

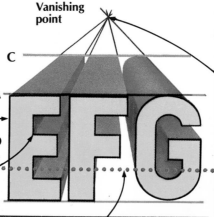

Vanishing point

1 Draw parallel guide lines (A and B) and then the letters.

5 Draw the outline and colour or ink in the letters.

4 Lightly join all points on the letters to the vanishing point.

3 Draw two lines (C and D) parallel to the guide lines, the depth you want the letters.

2 Mark a "vanishing point".

The lower the vanishing point, the more you appear to look up at the lettering.

The higher the vanishing point, the more you appear to look down.

---

*You can find out how to enlarge lettering on page 39.

Shadow letters

1 Draw parallel guide lines, shown in red. Draw the lettering as an outline between the top two.

2 Trace the lettering and superimpose it over the first outline, to line up with the bottom guide line.

3 Ink or colour in the sides of the letters, as shown in blue.

4 Draw in the pencil outlines in ink.

Distorted letters

1 Draw the letters, with a grid over them, as shown.

2 Draw a distorted grid freehand and sketch the letters to occupy the same proportion of each square of the grid.

3 Trace the sketch and fill in with ink or paint.

Number and letter the grid.

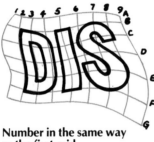

Number in the same way as the first grid.

Reversed

Draw or trace the letters in pencil as an outline.

Ink or colour in the background.

Two-point perspective

Use this method to draw 3-D letters which appear to be at an angle.

1 Draw a vertical line for the edge you want to appear nearest to you (leading edge).

Vanishing point

2 Mark the height you want.

3 Draw a base line.

4 Mark a point on the base line, called the vanishing point.

5 Join this vanishing point to the leading edge.

Vanishing point

6 Mark a second vanishing point.

Leading edge

7 Join the vanishing point to the leading edge.

8 Sketch your lettering between guide lines here.

9 Lightly project these lines to the first vanishing point.

10 Lightly project these lines to the second vanishing point.

11 Draw the outline and colour or ink in the letter. Erase the construction lines when the ink is dry.

3-D lettering

3-D letters are those with a raised or lowered surface and are used for signs, numbers, displays and so on. This page explains how to cut letters from different materials, such as card, polystyrene, wood, plaster and lino.

Card

You can make quite thick letters from corrugated card by gluing several pieces together. This process is called laminating.

1 Draw letters the size you want and trace onto corrugated card with carbon paper.

2 Repeat step 1 so there are enough pieces of card to make letters the thickness you want.

3 Cut out letters with a craft knife.

4 Glue, or laminate, letters together.

Glue on.

5 Fill the edges with Polyfilla*.

6 When dry, sandpaper and paint the edges.

7 Mount the letters on a backboard or stand.

22

Trade name for decorating filler.

Polystyrene

3-D letters can be made very quickly from polystyrene.

1 Carbon paper

 Draw letters the size you want and trace them onto polystyrene with carbon paper.

2 Knife

Cut around letters with a sharp knife using a sawing action.

Hot wire cutter

You can get special hot wire cutters which cut polystyrene very quickly and cleanly, but are expensive.

3 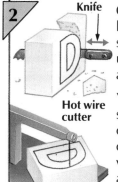 Paint the letters. Spray paint is ideal, but test a scrap first in case it melts the polystyrene.

4 Mount the letters on a backboard or base.

Glue

Wood

Use solid timber or marine plywood for permanent outdoor letters. Medium density fibreboard is ideal for indoors and is easy to cut.

1 Draw letters the size you want and trace them onto the wood with carbon paper.

2 Cut round letters with a jig saw, fret saw or band saw.

Jig saw	Fret saw	Band saw

3 To cut out the middle of letters, first drill a hole as shown, large enough to take the saw blade.

4 Finish letters by sanding and then polishing, varnishing or painting.

You may need screw holes to fix letters to a wall.

Carving letters

There are two kinds of carving – relief and incised. Relief letters are raised above the surface of the material; incised letters are cut into it.

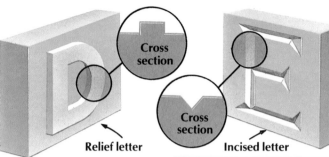

Relief letter

Cross section

Cross section

Incised letter

Lettering has been incised into many different materials since Palaeolithic times. The ancient Romans are considered by many experts to have produced the most beautiful stone inscriptions of all time.

Roman inscription

Materials

There are many materials you can use for carving: clay, stone, wood, plaster, lino – even chocolate.

For stone you need to buy proper chisels, but for softer materials you can use ordinary wood chisels and knives.

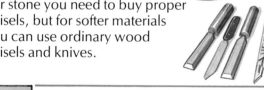

DESIGN TIPS

Lighting effects

You can alter the appearance of any 3-D lettering by lighting it differently.

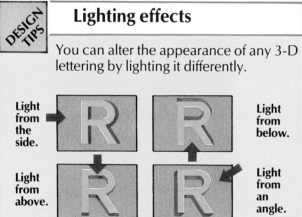

Light from the side.

Light from below.

Light from above.

Light from an angle.

Relief carving

Lino (from an art shop) is good for practising relief carving.

Draw the letters and transfer them to the lino with carbon paper.

Using lino cutters, gradually cut the material, working away from the edge of the letter.

Always work away from your fingers and eyes.

Finished lino-cut.

ABC

Incised letters

A block of plaster of Paris is good for practising incised lettering. You need a chisel and mallet.

Mallet

Chisel

Add plaster (about 5kg) to half a bowl of water until it forms a peak just above the surface. Mix thoroughly with the flat of your hand.

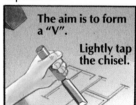

When hard, tip the plaster block out of the bowl.

1 Draw the letters and transfer them to the surface with carbon paper.

2 Cut the left side of the stem first, working upwards.

The aim is to form a "V".

Lightly tap the chisel.

3 Then cut the right side of the stem.

4 Cut the inside of curves first, starting near the narrowest part of the letter.

Cut serifs after this, if the style includes them.

Finished carving

Stencilling

Stencilled lettering is used mainly for functional purposes – labelling crates, for example – but it can also be used decoratively. There are two kinds of stencil: those you buy and those you make.

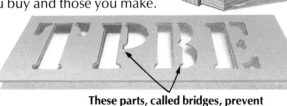

Stencilled crate

The letters in a stencil are reproduced by painting or drawing through the holes.

These parts, called bridges, prevent the letters from falling apart.

Making a stencil

1 Draw the lettering you want and glue it to a piece of card. This is called a cutting key.

2 Place a piece of stencil paper over the lettering and tape it down. Stencil paper is waxed, making it water resistant for painting.

Stencil paper

3 Cut through the paper, along the outline of each letter. Keep the blade at an angle to make an undercut so paint does not bleed under the stencil.

Blade must be sharp.

Cut each line in a single stroke.

Undercut

4 Either draw, spray or brush paint through the stencil. Be careful not to smudge the lettering when you lift the stencil.

Use a stiff brush like this.

Keep brush upright and dab it up and down.

Blunt end

For much larger lettering you could cut a stencil from cardboard.

There is a specially designed stencil alphabet to copy and use on page 40.

Cut paper lettering

Many famous artists have used cut coloured paper to make lettering, especially on collages. You can make collages by gluing lettering cut from coloured paper to a plain background.

How to cut letters

There are two ways of cutting letters, shown below.

1

This produces uneven, but lively letters.

Fix in your mind an idea of the shape you want and cut directly into the paper.

2
Draw the letters you want onto coloured paper and cut them out with a scalpel.

Another way of making letters from coloured paper is to cut strips and glue them edge on, as shown below.

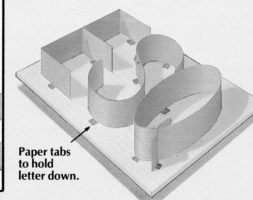

Paper tabs to hold letter down.

Rubbings

You can take rubbings on paper with wax crayon from any relief or incised lettering – manhole covers, coins, signs, inscriptions and so on.

Examples of rubbings.

1 Place the paper over the surface and rub with the crayon edge.

Keep paper still while rubbing.

Crayon

2 Different colour wax crayons.

An unusual way of lettering is to build up a library of rubbings, then cut them into individual letters to make alphabets.

3 Then paste letters together to make up words.

Spraying

Spray painting (or airbrushing) is a good way of creating fade effects like this.

Professional illustrators use an airbrush to create "chrome" effects like this.

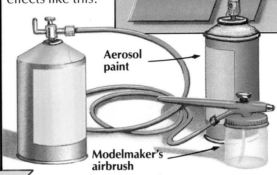

Aerosol paint

Modelmaker's airbrush

You can spray fade effects with cheap aerosol spray paints or modelmaker's airbrushes.

1 Draw the letters and trace them onto the surface you want to spray.

2 Stick masking film* over the letters and carefully cut round the outline without cutting the surface. You could cut a stencil instead, but masking film gives a better edge because the ink or paint is less likely to "bleed" under it.

Masking film

3 Spray the lightest colour first, keeping your hand moving while spraying. Let the colour dry.

4 Lightly spray the darker colour along the bottom edge as shown.

5 When the colour is dry, remove the masking film.

A thin plastic film, available from art shops, which sticks to the surface without damaging it when removed.

Typography

Typography has to do with organizing messages using, among other things, prefabricated characters. Originally typography was to do with printing, but it now applies to electronic methods of communication as well.

There have been many methods of making and setting (arranging) type, from metal through to the latest techniques using computers. All involve the use of standard, interchangeable characters.

Over the next six pages there are tips on using and getting type set. You can also find out how to identify different *typefaces* and how to use do-it-yourself type.

Hand set type. Each character to be printed used to be assembled by hand.

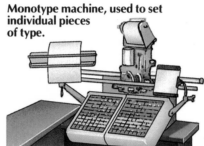

Monotype machine, used to set individual pieces of type.

Machine set type. In the 1880s Otto Mergenthaler developed a machine which set an entire line of type in molten metal.

Set of characters for phototypesetting.

Phototypesetting. In the last half century various machines have been invented which set type photographically onto paper. Later models incorporate computers.

The *copy* (words and other characters) is typed on a keyboard.

Copy can be corrected (edited) on the screen.

Digital typesetting. In the latest computer systems, characters are stored as digital codes. These are decoded and reproduced by computer-controlled laser onto photographic paper.

How to identify typefaces

There are so many typefaces that it is difficult to tell them apart. The one letter that usually gives away a typeface's identity is a small "g". Below are the "g"s of some popular typefaces.

g **Baskerville**	g **Garamond**	**g** **Eras**	g **Melior**	g **Bookman**	g **Bodoni**
g **Gill Sans**	g **Souvenir**	g **Plantin**	g **Helvetica**	g **Univers**	g **Perpetua**
g **Times roman**	g **Caslon Old Face**	g **Century Schoolbook**	g **Futura**	g **Rockwell**	g **Optima**

Typefaces and type designers

Some typefaces in use today were designed over four hundred yeas ago. Others are very recent.
Thousands of typefaces exist and more are being designed all the time. Here are some famous typefaces and their designers.

Caslon Old Face. Designed by William Caslon, 18th C.

abcdefghijklmnopqrstuv
ABCDEFGHIJKLMN
1234567890 123456789

Until this design, the best typefaces in England were imported from Holland.

Optima. Designed by Hermann Zapf, 1958.
Zapf based his design on ancient sans serif letters.

abcdefghijklmnopqrs
ABCDEFGHIJKLMNC
1234567890 1234567890

Optima is used in different sizes and weights for the text of this book.

Univers. Designed by Adrian Frutiger, 1950s.
Univers is a family of typefaces of different weights and widths.

abcdefghijklmnopqrs
ABCDEFGHIJKLMNC
1234567890 .,;:'"«»&

Univers met a demand for a new sans serif typeface.

Perpetua. Designed by Eric Gill, 1920s.
Gill named his design after a female saint, martyred in AD 203.

abcdefghijklmnopqrstuvwxy
ABCDEFGHIJK.MNOPQR
1234567890 123456789 .,;:'

This typeface was designed for the Monotype Corporation.

Bodoni. Based on types designed by Bodoni, late 18th C.

abcdefghijklmnopqrstu
ABCDEFGHIJKLMNC
1234567890 123456789

This is a "modern" typeface because of its strong contrasts of thicks and thins and its hair-line serifs.

Garamond. Designed by Jean Jannon, 17th C.
Garamonds are still popular typefaces today.

abcdefghijklmnopqrst
ABCDEFGHIJKLMNOI
1234567890 .,;:'"«»&!?

Called Garamond because it was thought to have been designed by him.

Futura. Designed by Paul Renner, 1928.
Futura is based on geometric shapes, repeated through the alphabet.

abcdefghijklmnopqrs
ABCDEFGHIJKLMNC
1234567890 .,;:'"«»&!

This typeface reflects the ideas of the modern movement in design of the period.

Other alphabets

Alphabets other than roman are also typeset. Below are four other alphabets and how to pronounce their letters.

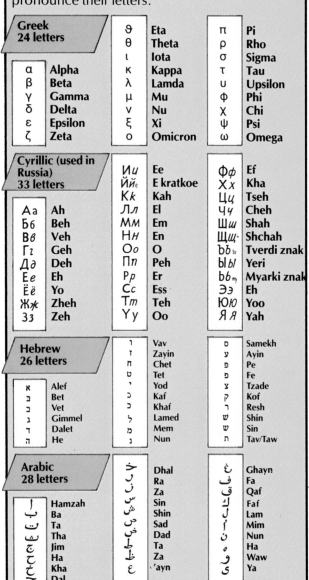

Greek 24 letters

α Alpha	ϑ/θ Eta		π Pi
β Beta	θ Theta		ρ Rho
γ Gamma	ι Iota		σ Sigma
δ Delta	κ Kappa		τ Tau
ε Epsilon	λ Lamda		υ Upsilon
ζ Zeta	μ Mu		φ Phi
	ν Nu		χ Chi
	ξ Xi		ψ Psi
	ο Omicron		ω Omega

Cyrillic (used in Russia) 33 letters

Аа Ah	Ии Ee		Фф Ef
Бб Beh	Йй Е kratkoe		Хх Kha
Вв Veh	Кк Kah		Цц Tseh
Гг Geh	Лл El		Чч Cheh
Дд Deh	Мм Em		Шш Shah
Ее Eh	Нн En		Щщ Shchah
Ёё Yo	Оо O		ъъ Tverdi znak
Жж Zheh	Пп Peh		ыы Yeri
Зз Zeh	Рр Er		ьь Myarki znak
	Сс Ess		Ээ Eh
	Тт Teh		Юю Yoo
	Уу Oo		Яя Yah

Hebrew 26 letters

א Alef	ו Vav		ס Samekh
ב Bet	ז Zayin		ע Ayin
ב Vet	ח Chet		פ Pe
ג Gimmel	ט Tet		פ Fe
ד Dalet	י Yod		צ Tzade
ה He	כ Kaf		ק Kof
	כ Khaf		ר Resh
	ל Lamed		ש Shin
	מ Mem		ש Sin
	נ Nun		ת Tav/Taw

Arabic 28 letters

Hamzah	Dhal		Ghayn
Ba	Ra		Fa
Ta	Za		Qaf
Tha	Sin		Faf
Jim	Shin		Lam
Ha	Sad		Mim
Kha	Dad		Nun
Dal	Ta		Ha
	Za		Waw
	'ayn		Ya

Numbers

There are two main kinds of numbers, shown below.

1234567890

◀ Old style (or non-ranging). The 3, 4, 5, 7 and 9 drop below the base line. The 6 and 8 extend above it.

Modern (or ranging). All the numbers line up between two lines. These look better with modern type styles. ▶

1234567890

Using type

These pages explain the typographical terms you need to know to turn *copy* (hand or typewritten words) into *typesetting*.

Measuring type

Three important measurements are used in typesetting. They are shown on the right with the special units used to measure them.

1 Height of the body of the type, called the type size (measured in points but sometimes in millimetres).

2 The distance between one line of type and another (measured from baseline to baseline in points or millimetres).

Making pots on a potter's wheel is called "throwing". The name describes how the clay is thrown outwards by the force of the rotating wheel. By controlling this force you can make a huge range of shapes.

3 Column width, called the line length or measure (measured in picas or millimetres).

Type size

Two systems are used to measure type: the Anglo-American *point* (English speaking countries), and the *Didot* point (Europe). The Didot point is slightly larger than the Anglo-American point.

Millimetres are also used, but usually only for large sizes.

Anglo-American point

12 points = 1 pica
1 point = approx. 1/72in
1 pica   12×1/72in=1/6in.

72pt

Size of type in points.

The size of type is usually expressed in points.

The Didot point

12 points = 1 cicero
1 point = 0.376mm
1 cicero = 4.5111mm

72pt

Size of type in points.

The x-height

Different type styles, all of the same point size, may look large or small when compared with one another. This is because their *x-heights* are not the same.

Garamond   Times roman

X   X

30pt type   30pt type

Line feed

Line feed is the distance between one line of type and another, measured from baseline to baseline. It used to be called leading, when a strip of metal was inserted between lines of type to make a gap.

Type can be set closely or with additional line feed.

Closely set lines of type.

y had a little lamb
fleece was white as snow
everywhere that Mary went

y had a little lamb
fleece was white as snow
everywhere that Mary went

Lines with 2 point extra line feed.

Calculating depth

Special "rulers" called *depth scales* are used to calculate the depth of type of different sizes.

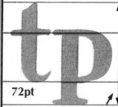

Depth scale

Each column represents one size of type.

Other sizes are marked on the back.

This example shows how to work out the depth of a column of 6 lines of type of a certain size.

10/12pt type (said as, "10 on 12 point"). This means 10pt type on a 12pt line feed.

Ignore the type size – use the bottom figure as it gives the line feed. Using the 12 point scale, mark where shown.

This is the depth of 6 lines of any typeface set on 12pt lines.

Type set with the size of the type the same as the line feed is written like this

11/11pt.

Line lengths

Type is set in two main ways: *justified* and *unjustified*.

Justified type	Unjustified type
Hey diddle diddle the cat had a fiddle the cow jumped over the moon	Hey diddle diddle the cat had a fiddle the cow jumped over the moon

The line length is the maximum width, called the measure, of a line of type. It is measured in picas, *ciceros*, or millimetres (see below).

You can use the 12pt part of a depth scale to measure type widthways. This is because 12 points = 1 pica/cicero.

Pica depth scale

This example shows the width of 10 picas of any size of type.

Marking up

Marking up means writing instructions on your copy for the typesetter to follow. Special codes are used in the margin, as shown in the chart below.

Ital /	Italics
BF /	Bold
CAP /	Capitals
A /	New paragraph
# /	Insert space
⌒	Close up gap
⅃ /	Move type to the right
⌐ /	Move type to the left
Trs	Transpose words
no A /	Run on (no new paragraph)
Y	Delete (remove)
/	Insert new words

Here is an example of marked-up copy.

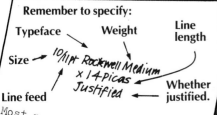

Remember to specify:

Typeface · Weight · Line length
Size → 10/11pt Rockwell Medium × 14 Picas Justified
Line feed · Whether justified.

Most people like to take a holiday at least once a year. A very popular destination this year is the Coa...
What i...

Ems

An em is a square the size of a typeface's point size.

12pts
12pt em ← 12pts
36pts
36pt em → 36pts

A 12 point em is often used as a measurement of width, since a 12 point em is the same width as 1 pica.

12pt em ▪ = 1 pica ▪

Copy fitting

Copy fitting (or casting off) means calculating how much space copy will occupy when typeset in a certain typeface and size. This example shows one method of copy fitting.

Typewritten copy

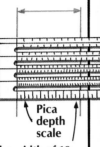

Once upon a time
there was an aard
called Androcles.
lived in an enorn
palace, where he
spent most of his
time lazing aroun
the sun. Sadly,
there were no oth
aardvarks around
company, so poor
Androcles was qui
lonely.

Once upon a time aardvark called A an enormous pala ... f his ...

Same copy in 10/11pt

Once upon a time there wa lived in an enormous palac lazing around in the sun. Sa around for comp... ...

Same copy in 6/7pt

1 Find the total number of characters by multiplying the average number per line by the number of lines of text.

Count spaces and punctuation marks as characters.

there was an aardva
called Androcles.
lived in an enormo
palace, w **243 characters**

2 Decide on the measure (width) you want to use.

8 PICAS
10 PICAS
12 PICAS

This grid has columns 13 picas wide.

3 Decide on the typeface and size.

10/11pt Eras
abcdefghijklmnopqrstu
ABCDEFGHIJKLMNO
1234567890 .,;;'' «» &.!?

4 Divide the total number of characters in the text by the number of characters per line. Typesetters supply specimen sheets with tables showing characters per pica for sizes of type.

Point size				Width of column		
Picas	10	11	12	13	14	15
8pt	31	35	39	43	47	51
9pt	30	33	36	39	42	45
10pt	29	31	33	35	37	39

Number of characters

37 characters in 14 picas

243 ÷ 37 = 6.56 lines

5 Round up to the nearest whole number and mark off the depth with a depth scale.

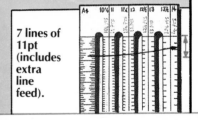

7 lines of 11pt (includes extra line feed).

If the typesetting comes out too long, start again with:

*A smaller type size, or
*Wider columns, or
*Smaller line feed, or
*Less copy

If the typesetting is too short, try:

*A larger type size, or
*Narrower columns, or
*Greater line feed, or
*Add pictures, or
*Leave spaces

Designing with type

This page gives some tips on things to take into account when designing with type.

Display and text type

Typefaces are designed for two different uses: those for large blocks of *copy* are called text, or book, faces; those for headings and titles are called display faces.

Display faces

CHARMMA

COMPASS

Bloody Horror

SLIPSTREAM

Many more display faces have been designed than text faces.	Display faces are usually 14 points or larger.

Text faces

Optima

Times

Univers

Baskerville

Text faces are sometimes used for headings too, as in this book.

Impact

Headings have most impact when set with the first letter as a capital and the rest as small letters. Capitals join visually top and bottom.

Man eating monster feels ill

MAN EATING MONSTER FEELS ILL

Size

Choose a type size appropriate to your message and audience. The further away the message is to be read, the larger the typeface must be, for example.

Beware of the drop

Once upon a time

Type weight

The boldness of a typeface is called its weight.

Eras light
Eras book
Eras medium
Eras semi bold
Eras bold

For text, it is usually best not to use too bold a typeface.

Legibility

Legibility means how easy or difficult something is to read. There are many things that affect legibilty; some are explained below.

- *Sans serif* is thought to be less easy to read than *serif* type. This may be because some sans serif letters look more similar to one another than letters with serifs do, unlike those with serifs.

I must go down to the sea again, to the lonely sea and the sky, I left my shoes and socks there, I wonder if they're dry? **Serif**	I must go down to the sea again, to the lonely sea and the sky, I left my shoes and socks there, I wonder if they're dry ? **Sans serif**

- Large areas of text set in capitals takes longer to read than those set in small letters.

Lucy Legwarmer, aged 8, was first on the scene when her dog Spike pinned the burglar against the wall.	LUCY LEGWARMER, AGED 8, WAS FIRST ON THE SCENE WHEN HER DOG SPIKE PINNED THE BURGLAR AGAINST THE WALL.

- Very short and very long lines of type are hard to read.

  Very few people realize how difficult it is to parachute onto the top of a skyscraper.

  Very few people realize how difficult it is to parachute onto the top of a skyscraper.

- It is best to choose only one or two type styles for a design, but to have some variation in type weight.

  For Sale
  Turbo-powered Spacecraft.
  Hardly used. Good fuel consumption. Complete with instructions.
  Phone 456739

Do-it-yourself type

You can do your own "typesetting" with instant lettering, typewriters and word processors.

Rub-down lettering

Instant rub-down lettering is ideal for headings and short messages.

Sheet of rub-down lettering.

Draw in light blue if the lettering is for printing.

Guide line

Spacing marks

1

Draw two guide lines: one where you want the lettering, the other in line with the space marks on the sheet.

2

Rub down space mark too.

Special tool or blunt end of pencil.

Remove the backing sheet and align the spacing marks below the letter you want on the lower blue line. Rub the letter with a tool until it appears grey.

3

Align the mark below the next letter so that it butts up against the first mark. Rub down both letter and mark.

4

Carefully remove all the spacing marks by lifting them with a piece of masking tape.

You can also use masking tape to remove mistakes.

5

Place the backing sheet over the lettering and fix them in place by rubbing with a tool.

6

Repair any damaged letters with a black pen.

7
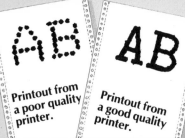

Layout

If necessary, cut the lettering and paste it into position on your layout.

Word processors

Most word processors give a choice between printing justified or unjustified text. The quality of printers varies enormously.

Printout from a poor quality printer.

Printout from a good quality printer.

Typewriters

Typewritten copy can be made to look good enough for printing, especially if you use a carbon ribbon rather than an ordinary cotton one.

Cotton ribbon	ABCDE
Carbon ribbon	ABCDE

You can create *justified* text with an ordinary typewriter like this:

1 Set the tab* to give the number of characters you want across a column.

2 Type the copy, with stars to fill up the end of each line.

```
Many years ago in a*
damp and smelly cave
in the woods, there*
lived a sad old*****
goblin called Fred.*
```

3 Re-type the copy with extra spaces between the words to take up the number of spaces at the end of each line.

```
Many  years ago in a
damp and smelly cave
in the  woods, there
lived    a   sad old
goblin  called Fred.
```

Typewritten copy looks best reduced by 15%-25%, as this makes some of the irregularities in the spacing less obvious.

Reduced typewritten copy

```
ago in a
lly cave
s, there
sad old
ed Fred.
ry old
```

```
ars ago in a
smelly cave
woods, there
a  sad old
called Fred
```

*This sets the length of a line of typing.

Page design

Any printed or written message, from books and magazines to exhibition panels and advertisements, needs to be organized in some way. This is popularly called *layout*. Good layout is the result of careful arrangement of all *graphic elements* in a message.

This page explains the technical words used to describe the layout of a magazine. The same applies to any kind of message, but not all the features shown need be used. You can also find out about layout design techniques.

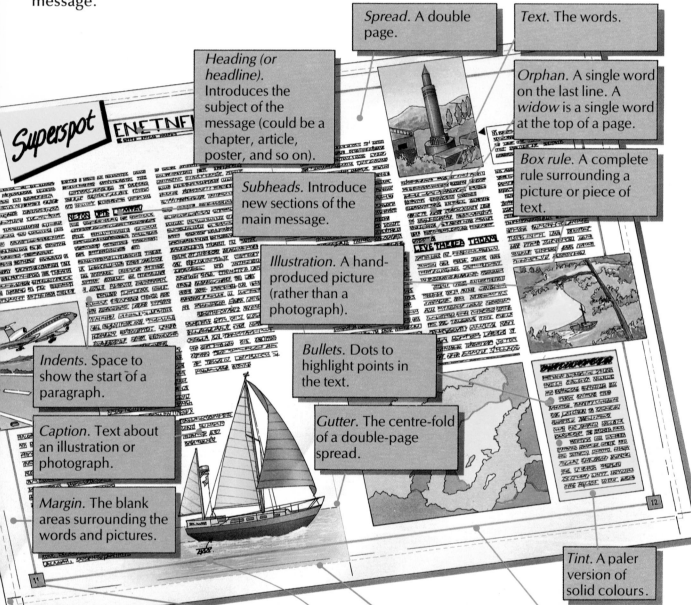

Spread. A double page.

Text. The words.

Heading (or headline). Introduces the subject of the message (could be a chapter, article, poster, and so on).

Orphan. A single word on the last line. A *widow* is a single word at the top of a page.

Box rule. A complete rule surrounding a picture or piece of text.

Subheads. Introduce new sections of the main message.

Illustration. A hand-produced picture (rather than a photograph).

Indents. Space to show the start of a paragraph.

Bullets. Dots to highlight points in the text.

Gutter. The centre-fold of a double-page spread.

Caption. Text about an illustration or photograph.

Margin. The blank areas surrounding the words and pictures.

Tint. A paler version of solid colours.

Trim or crop marks. Marks outside the page showing where the paper is to be cut.

Folio. Page number.

Label. A very short caption, often with an arrow.

Bleed. Where an illustration or photograph goes over the outside margin and off the edge of the page.

Rules. Horizontal and vertical lines, often used to divide up parts of the message.

Grids

A *grid* is like an invisible framework within which pages of books, magazines and so on are designed.

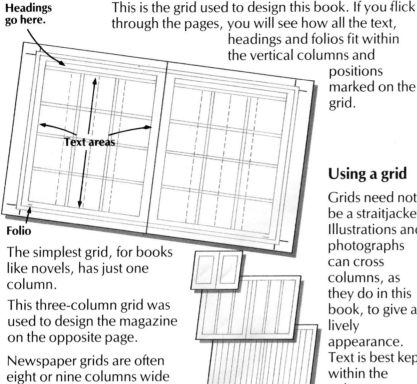

Headings go here.

Text areas

Folio

This is the grid used to design this book. If you flick through the pages, you will see how all the text, headings and folios fit within the vertical columns and positions marked on the grid.

The simplest grid, for books like novels, has just one column.

This three-column grid was used to design the magazine on the opposite page.

Newspaper grids are often eight or nine columns wide for each page.

Using a grid

Grids need not be a straitjacket. Illustrations and photographs can cross columns, as they do in this book, to give a lively appearance. Text is best kept within the columns.

Drawing a grid

If you want to design a magazine, comic or something similar, it is a good idea to draw a grid first.

Decide on the size, or format, you need.

Using a ruler and set square (or drawing board and T-square if you have them), draw in the outside edges of the page.

Use a light blue pencil as this will not show if the page is copied for printing.

Draw in the columns and any other guide lines needed.

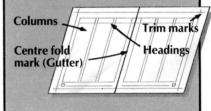

Columns

Trim marks

Centre fold mark (Gutter)

Headings

Electronic page layout

Some design studios use computers to design layouts. A design idea is gradually built up on the screen using the real text and pictures.

Printer

Electronic page layout software is available for many home computers.

Drawing layouts

DESIGN TIPS

Grids are essential for drawing layouts, as they help you to decide where to put things.*

Use your best sketch to refine your ideas by tracing over it. Continue this process until the layout is ready to draw neatly.

▼ **Professional designers use this technique.**

Layout paper

Grid

▲ Slip your grid under tracing or layout paper to sketch ideas for a layout.

Felt pens and markers are good for layouts.

Sketch

*See pages 26-27 to find out how to work out how much space type will occupy.

Designing an alphabet

These pages show how Michael Harvey, a well-known lettering designer, created an alphabet for this book.*

Designers go through several stages when designing a new alphabet, and you can see these at work here.

Stage 1 / Brief

Designers usually work to a brief – instructions setting out what the customer, or client, wants.

The brief here was to design a multi-purpose stencil alphabet, and to suggest some possible uses.

Stage 2 / Ideas and inspiration

Designers get their ideas from many sources – often by adapting an existing idea – and many keep files and sketch books of reference material that might be useful.

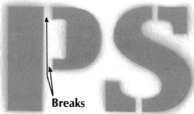

Breaks

ABCDEFGH
IJKLMNOP
QRSTUVW
XYZ &?!., **Egyptian**

Design briefs usually impose constraints of some kind. For example, a stencil has to have bridges in the letterforms or it will fall apart. Constraints like this help the designer to decide what to do.

Inspiration for the alphabet came from looking at road markings, and also at a 19th century letterform, called Egyptian. Stencil letters are often based on bold styles with heavy *serifs*.

Stage 3 / Try-outs

Next, the designer made a series of sketches to develop his ideas.

Drawn letter, based closely on the original Egyptian.

Freehand drawing, with shaped strokes and fewer serifs.

Idea 3 The designer decided to try combining written letterforms with the original Egyptian style to make it look more elegant.

Each letter was built up, stroke by stroke, with a broad pen.

This is how it looked.

W X

ABCDEFGHIJKLM
NOPQRSTUVWXYZ

The letters were then drawn freehand, removing the lower serifs to improve the way they fit together.

Stage 4 — Master drawings

Master drawings, from which copies can be taken, are carefully drawn in outline on a large scale, using drawing instruments.

All parts of the letters – stems, serifs, curves – must be consistent in weight and detail from letter to letter. The letters must be drawn to work well together in any arrangement of words.

The complete alphabet drawn in outline.

At this stage, the alphabet can be enlarged or reduced photographically. A process called PMT (photo mechanical transfer) is often used to do this*.

Stage 5 — Stencils and uses

Michael Harvey suggested two uses for the alphabet: to make a road marking for a private parking space and for stencilling children's wooden alphabet blocks.

Alphabet enlarged and traced onto cardboard for a road-marking stencil.

White paint for outside use.

Alphabet traced onto waxed stencil paper to make wooden alphabet blocks.

DESIGN TIPS — Designing alphabets

Here are some points to take into account if you want to design your own alphabet.

*Parts of letters, like serifs and stems, should normally look the same for every letter in the alphabet.

*It is easier to keep details consistent if you work on groups of similar shaped letters, rather than go from A-Z.

LHTLEF
AVWYX
KMNZ
OQCGDUJ
PRBS
Lhnmrut
vnyxkz
ocedqpb
agsfij

*All letters must be either upright or slanted at the same angle.

Designing a message

Messages should be designed so as to communicate successfully their content.

These pages give tips on planning a message. To do this you first need to think about the following:

- its purpose,
- the people for whom it is intended,
- how it will be used,
- the reproduction facilities at your disposal.

The chart below shows the main kinds of messages and suggests how you might approach them.

News

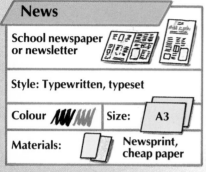

School newspaper or newsletter

Style: Typewritten, typeset

Colour		Size:	A3

Materials: Newsprint, cheap paper

Instruction

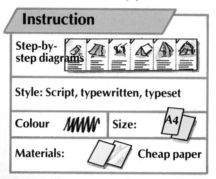

Step-by-step diagrams

Style: Script, typewritten, typeset

Colour		Size:	A4

Materials: Cheap paper

Information

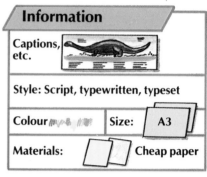

Captions, etc.

Style: Script, typewritten, typeset

Colour		Size:	A3

Materials: Cheap paper

Display

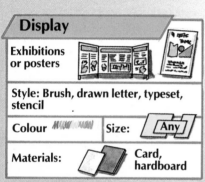

Exhibitions or posters

Style: Brush, drawn letter, typeset, stencil

Colour		Size:	Any

Materials: Card, hardboard

Advertisement

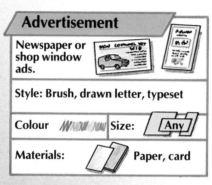

Newspaper or shop window ads.

Style: Brush, drawn letter, typeset

Colour		Size:	Any

Materials: Paper, card

Direction

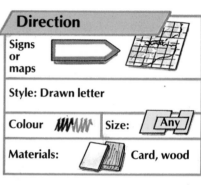

Signs or maps

Style: Drawn letter

Colour		Size:	Any

Materials: Card, wood

Identification

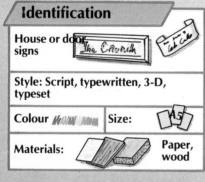

House or door signs

Style: Script, typewritten, 3-D, typeset

Colour		Size:	A5

Materials: Paper, wood

Warning

Danger signs or medicine labels

Style: Drawn letter, brush, stencil

Colour		Size:	Any

Materials: Card, wood

Announcement

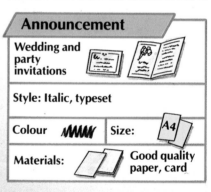

Wedding and party invitations

Style: Italic, typeset

Colour		Size:	A4

Materials: Good quality paper, card

Celebration

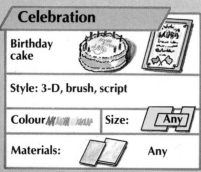

Birthday cake

Style: 3-D, brush, script

Colour		Size:	Any

Materials: Any

Presentation

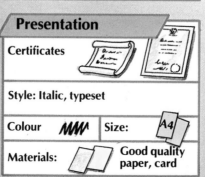

Certificates

Style: Italic, typeset

Colour		Size:	A4

Materials: Good quality paper, card

Story

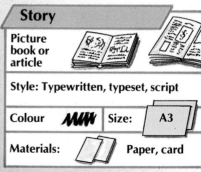

Picture book or article

Style: Typewritten, typeset, script

Colour		Size:	A3

Materials: Paper, card

Printing methods

In case you want to reproduce your work, various printing methods are explained below.

Photocopying D.I.Y.

Up to 50 copies

Access. Libraries and instant print shops.

Reasonable quality text. Some pictures may suffer.

Colour available, but expensive.

Up to A3 size

Stencil duplicating D.I.Y.

A stencil duplicator forces ink through a stencil onto paper.

Up to 3,000 copies

Access. Schools, instant print shops, community groups.

Fair quality text and black line drawings.

A4 size.

Screen printing D.I.Y.

Screen printing is a type of stencil printing, in which ink of any colour is forced through a screen onto paper with a rubber blade (called a "squeegee").

Very slow.

Excellent results with large solid areas of colour, but not small text.

Up to A2 size.

Can print on any flat surface (e.g. T-shirts, wood, plastic, card).

Access. Schools and community groups. Art shops sell cheap kits.

Commercial printing

There are many types of commercial printing available for professional quality work. Most towns have instant print shops.

Understand the problem

Whether designing a poster for a charity sale or a magazine, the first priority is to understand the message and its purpose.

Brief

Read the message (along with any brief you may have) and break it down into its main components.

Copy

Ring the components. Number the components according to their order of importance.

These components are of equal importance, so are given the same number.

Each component needs to be made to look separate and more or less important than the other parts.

Thumbnail sketches (see page 7) are a good way of trying out different ideas.

Making things stand out

DESIGN TIPS

There are lots of design elements you can use to make parts of a message stand out, shown below. But things usually stand out most when they are different.

Size:
The biggest burger in the world!

Boldness:
Learn to ride a **Wheeler** bike.

Italic:
Suddenly, Lizzie saw a *huge* spider.

Underscore:
Congratulations on your birthday.

Devices:
*Aunty Flo *Cousin Spike

Directional elements:
Now turn the page →

Colour:
The colour this year is red

Borders:
Bike for sale | Very cheap |

Capitals:
Take a trip to KENYA

Different style:
Live performance by **Track**

Slant:
Don't lose your way.

Isolation:
Phil Over   The star

Decorated or large initial:
Claude Back, the lion tamer

Reversed lettering:
Black and white

Coloured background:
Sponsored fun run

Condensed type:
It was a tight squeeze

Expanded type:
Everyone spread out

Distortion:
Spike blew a BUBBLE

Descriptive lettering:
CRASH

You can use one or a combination of these techniques to emphasize the most important parts of your message. But don't overdo things.

Paste-up

Paste-up is the process of assembling all the components of a design – *typesetting* or hand-lettering and any *pictures* – ready for printing.

This page shows how to do paste-up which includes line illustrations to be printed in black.

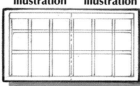

Line illustration	Tone illustration	Colour illustration

Grid drawn on thin card.

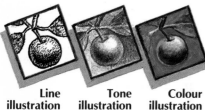

For paste-up you need a *grid* (see page 33) drawn in blue pencil.

1

First take photocopies of all the components for the page or spread and cut them up.

2

Trace main outlines of grid.

Slip the grid under tracing paper and stick the copies in place to make sure everything fits. Remove the grid.

3

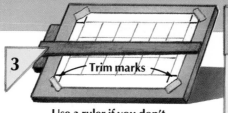

Use a ruler if you don't have a T-square.

If you have a drawing board, tape the grid to it and use a T-square to draw trim marks on it in black ink.

4

Carefully trim the originals to within about 3mm of the edge.

5

Apply glue to the back of each piece.

6

Make sure each piece is straight by using a T-square or ruler.

Carefully position each piece on the grid according to your rough paste-up.

7

Re-check for straightness by looking end-on across the page. Cover the paste-up with paper to protect it.

DESIGN TIPS — Optical illusions

In lettering you often need to distort apparently correct proportions to compensate for optical illusions.

*All curved and pointed parts of letters should extend beyond the guide lines.

These letters will look too small if drawn within the guide lines.

If you sit curved parts on the guidelines, the letters will look too small.

*In styles with thick and thin strokes, the widest part of curves is thicker than the thickest stem of a straight letter. This avoids it looking too thin.

*Diagonal strokes may need to be thinner towards the point at which they meet.

Diagonal strokes may need to be thinner than vertical strokes, or they can look too heavy.

*The stem strokes of capitals must be thicker than those of small letters.

*The centre bars of B, E, F and H need to be slightly above the true centre to avoid looking too low.

Copying alphabets

On the next four pages are alphabets to copy and use. You may also want to copy other alphabets. First trace the letters you want and then enlarge or reduce them.

Tracing

Trace the letters you want as shown below.

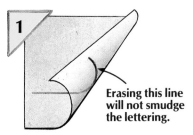

On the back of a piece of tracing paper, draw a guide line in pencil.

Trace the letters to make up the words you want.

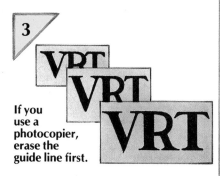

If you use a photocopier, erase the guide line first.

Enlarge or reduce the lettering to the size you want, either by the grid method (shown on the right) or by using a photocopier with enlarging/reducing facilities.

Grid enlarging

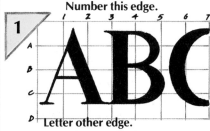

Number this edge.
1 2 3 4 5 6 7
A
B
C
D
Letter other edge.

Draw a grid over the lettering as shown.

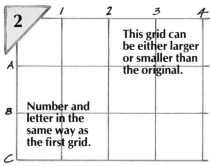

1 2 3 4
A
B
C

This grid can be either larger or smaller than the original.

Number and letter in the same way as the first grid.

Draw another grid the size you want the lettering to be.

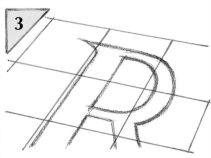

Use the grid lines as a guide to drawing the letters freehand.

Paint or ink in the lettering as shown on page 18.

Making a lettering sheet

You may want to use letters of the same size for lots of different things. A lettering sheet is a quick way of doing this. The steps below show how to make one.

AAAAABBBCCCC
DDDDEEEEEEFFF
GGGHHHHIIIIIJJK
KLLLLMMM NNN
N NOOOOOPPPQ
Q RRRRRSSSSSTT
TTTUUUUVVWW
WXX YYYZZ

Letters are repeated according to the frequency of their use in English.

Trace and enlarge the alphabet you want as shown below to make a master sheet.

Take photocopies of the master sheet.

THR
OP

Don't cut up the master sheet.

Cut up letters as needed and paste them together to compose words.

Either take a copy or trace off the lettering and ink or colour it as you want.

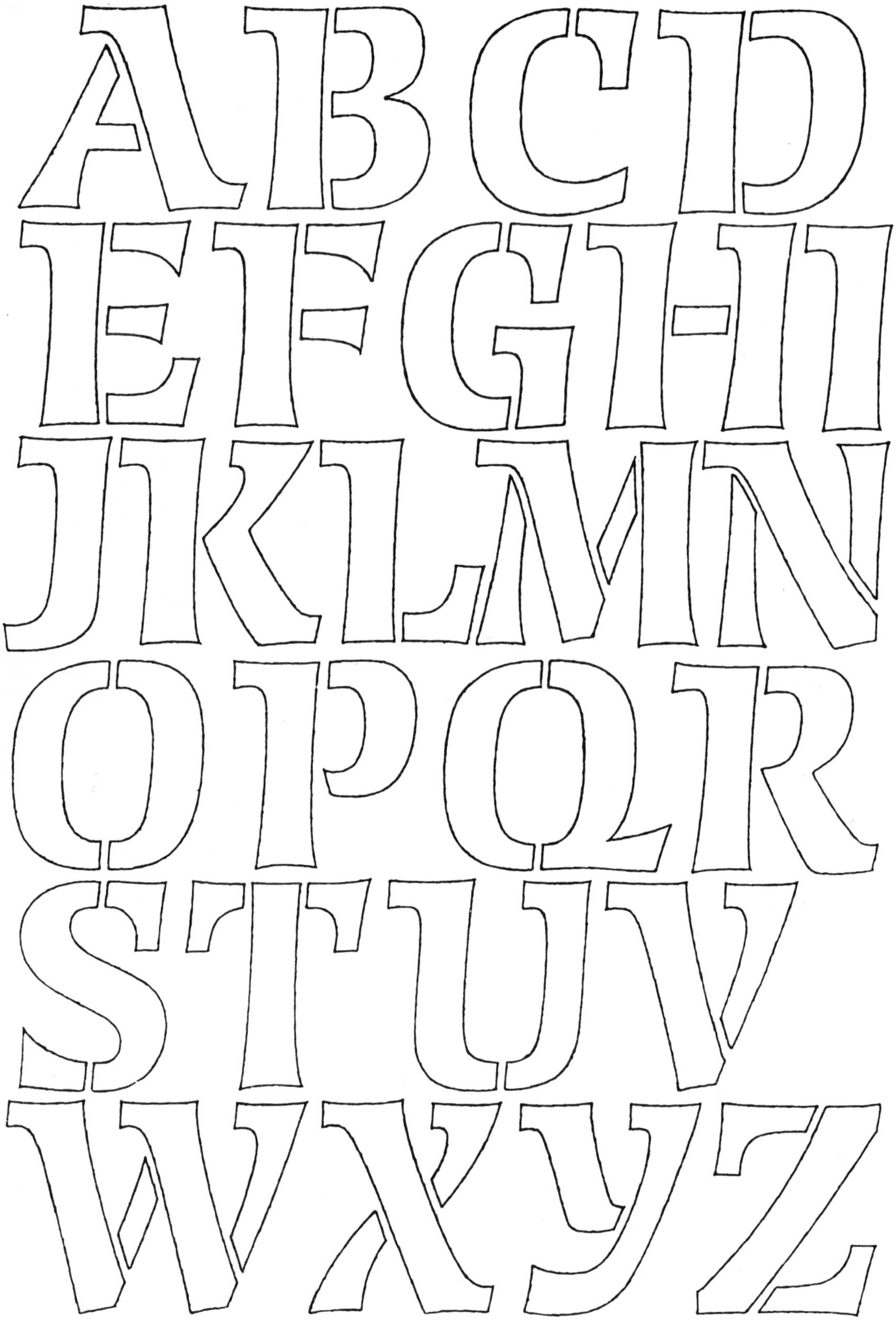

ABCD
EFGH
JKLMN
OPQR
STUV
WXYZ

HARVEY STENCIL Designed by Michael Harvey 1986

abcdefghijklmn
opqrstuvwxyz
ABCDEFGHIJ
KLMNOPQRS
TUVWXYZ
1234567890
?!&£$.,:;-'""

abcdefghijkl
mnopqrstuv
wxyzABCDE
FGHIJKLMN
OPQRSTUV
WXYZ12345
67890?!'",£&

CUMBRIA Designed by Wilf Dickie 1986

ABCDEFGH
IJKLMNOPQ
RSTUVWX
YZ&.,:;'"""!?
-()-*/%$¢12
34567890

COMPASS CASUAL

abcdefghijklm
nopqrstuvw
xyz ABCDEF
GHIJKLMNO
PQRSTUVW
XYZ 12345678
90:;,.‟?!$£"(%)

PALATINO Designed by Hermann Zapf 1950

abcdefghijkl
mnopqrstuv
wxyz ABCD
EFGHIJKLM
NOPQRSTU
VWXYZ
1234567890
:;,."?!\$£"(%)

Equipment and materials

Below is a list of the basic equipment and materials mentioned in this book. You can buy all these things from art shops and some stationers.

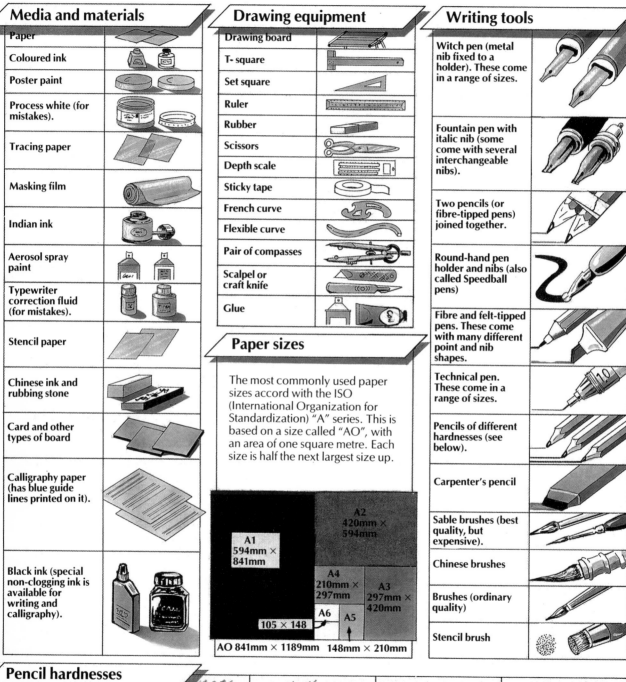

Media and materials

- Paper
- Coloured ink
- Poster paint
- Process white (for mistakes).
- Tracing paper
- Masking film
- Indian ink
- Aerosol spray paint
- Typewriter correction fluid (for mistakes).
- Stencil paper
- Chinese ink and rubbing stone
- Card and other types of board
- Calligraphy paper (has blue guide lines printed on it).
- Black ink (special non-clogging ink is available for writing and calligraphy).

Drawing equipment

- Drawing board
- T- square
- Set square
- Ruler
- Rubber
- Scissors
- Depth scale
- Sticky tape
- French curve
- Flexible curve
- Pair of compasses
- Scalpel or craft knife
- Glue

Paper sizes

The most commonly used paper sizes accord with the ISO (International Organization for Standardization) "A" series. This is based on a size called "AO", with an area of one square metre. Each size is half the next largest size up.

A1 594mm × 841mm
A2 420mm × 594mm
A4 210mm × 297mm
A3 297mm × 420mm
A6 105 × 148
A5
AO 841mm × 1189mm   148mm × 210mm

Writing tools

- Witch pen (metal nib fixed to a holder). These come in a range of sizes.
- Fountain pen with italic nib (some come with several interchangeable nibs).
- Two pencils (or fibre-tipped pens) joined together.
- Round-hand pen holder and nibs (also called Speedball pens)
- Fibre and felt-tipped pens. These come with many different point and nib shapes.
- Technical pen. These come in a range of sizes.
- Pencils of different hardnesses (see below).
- Carpenter's pencil
- Sable brushes (best quality, but expensive).
- Chinese brushes
- Brushes (ordinary quality)
- Stencil brush

Pencil hardnesses

7B Very soft	4B	B	H	4H
6B	3B	HB Medium	2H	5H
5B	2B	F	3H	6H Very hard

Glossary

Artwork. Lettering and/or pictures ready for reproduction.

Ascender. A stroke extending above the main part *(x height)* of a small letter.

Base line. The imaginary line on which letters and other characters appear to sit.

Bleed. Where an *illustration* or photograph extends beyond a cut edge of a page.

Box rule. A line drawn round *text* and/or pictures.

Bullet. Dots to highlight points in the *text.*

Calligraphy. Literally, "beautiful writing".

Caption. Text accompanying an *illustration* or photograph.

Cicero. A unit of measurement used in *typography* in Europe. 12 *Didot points* = 1 cicero.

Construction line. Lightly drawn pencil line.

Copy. The particular version of a *text* used for *typesetting.*

Copy fitting (or casting off). The preliminary measurement of *copy* to estimate the space it will occupy in a given size of type.

Depth scale. A special ruler marked in *point* sizes, used to measure the depth of a given number of lines of *typesetting.*

Descender. A stroke extending below the main part *(x height)* of a small letter.

Didot point. A unit of measurement used in *typography* in Europe. 1 Didot *point* = 0.376mm.

Em. The square of any given type size. The 12pt em *(pica em)* is used for linear measurements.

Folio. A page number.

Font/fount (or character set). A complete set of characters of a particular type size.

Graphic element. Any component part of a message, e.g. letter, *rule, illustration* and so on.

Grid. The framework of lines marking the margins and columns of a page and used as an aid in designing.

Gutter. The margins where two pages meet at a fold.

Heading (or headline). A title that draws attention to part of a *text.*

Illustration. A hand-produced picture.

Indent. A blank space at the beginning of a line, usually at the start of a paragraph or other item.

Justified. Lines of type of the same length, making straight-sided columns.

Label. A very short *caption,* often with an arrow.

Layout (page design). A plan showing the arrangement of words and pictures.

Line feed. The distance between lines of *text,* measured from *base line* to base line.

Margin. The outer blank areas surrounding the words and pictures.

Marking up. Writing instructions on *copy* for *typesetting.*

Orphan. A short line or single word at the foot of a page or column of *text.*

Paste-up. The process of assembling *text* and pictures ready for reproduction.

Pica. A unit of linear measurement used in *typography.* 12 *points* = 1 pica.

Point. The traditional unit of measurement in *typography.* 12 points = 1 pica (or *cicero).*

Rule. Horizontal and vertical lines, often used to divide up parts of the message.

Run-around. Type set to fit around the edge of a picture.

Sans serif (or sanserif). Type without *serifs.*

Serif. Strokes which finish off the ends of a letter's stems, arms and other parts.

Spread. Two pages side by side.

Subhead. A secondary level of *heading.*

Text. The words.

Tint. A coloured area, composed of minute dots or lines to produce a paler version of a solid colour.

Trim (or crop marks). Marks outside the page showing where the paper is to be cut.

Typeface. The name for a particular design of type.

Typesetting. The process of assembling type to form words.

Typography. The study and design of printed and other graphic messages.

Unjustified. Text setting in which the column of lines is straight on one side and irregular on the other.

Widow. A short line at the head of a page or column.

x height. The height of a small x.

Going further

Some useful books to read are suggested below.

Creative Lettering, Michael Harvey, The Bodley Head, 1985

Lettering Tips, Bill Gray, Van Nostrand Reinhold, 1983

Tips on Type, Bill Gray, Van Nostrand Reinhold, 1983

The Complete Guide to Calligraphy, Judy Martin, Phaidon, 1984

The Alternative Printing Handbook, Chris Treweek and Jonathan Zeitlyn, Penguin, 1983

Mastering Calligraphy, Tom Gourdie, Search Press, 1984

Lettering Techniques, John Lancaster, Batsford, 1982

Calligraphy Techniques, John Lancaster, Batsford, 1986

Layout and Design for Calligraphers, Alan Furber, Dryad Press, 1985

Typography, Ruari McLean, Thames and Hudson, 1980

Manual of Graphic Techniques 3, Tom Porter and Sue Goodman, Astragal Books, 1983

Answers to puzzle on page 4

1 Eras
2 Century Schoolbook
3 Gill Sans
4 Melior

Index